The Rise of Nvidia

How the ChipMaker Surpassed Apple to become the Second Largest Publicly Traded Company in the US and its impact on AI and Tech Industries.

Brent T. Lowe

Copyright©2024 [Brent T. Lowe]

All rights reserved. No part of this publication may be reproduced, distributed, or transmitted in any form or by any means, including photocopying, recording, or other electronic or mechanical methods, without the prior written permission of the publisher, except in the case of brief quotations embodied in critical reviews and certain other noncommercial uses permitted by copyright law.

TABLE OF CONTENT

Introduction 5

Chapter 1 9
   The Early Days 9

Chapter 2 17
   The Evolution of Chip Technology 17

Chapter 3 25
   Entering the AI Revolution 25

Chapter 4 33
   Breaking New Grounds: Key Milestones 33

Chapter 5 39
   Financial Growth and Market Strategy 39

Chapter 6 45
   Competition and Market Dynamics 45

Chapter 7 51
   AI and Deep Learning: The Game Changers 51

Chapter 8 57
   Surpassing Apple: A Historic Milestone 57

Chapter 9 61
   Technological Innovations and Patents 61

Chapter 10 65
   The Rubin Platform and Beyond 65

Chapter 11 69
   Corporate Culture and Leadership 69
Chapter 12 73
   Global Impact and Market Presence 73
Chapter 13 77
   The Future of Nvidia and AI 77
   Conclusion 81

Introduction

Nvidia's rise from a modest startup to a global tech powerhouse is one of the most remarkable stories in the modern technology landscape. Founded in 1993 by Jensen Huang, Chris Malachowsky, and Curtis Priem, Nvidia began with a clear vision: to build the best graphics card for the burgeoning personal computer market. Over the decades, this vision expanded, propelling Nvidia to the forefront of not just graphics processing units (GPUs) but also artificial intelligence (AI) and deep learning technologies, fundamentally transforming multiple industries along the way.

Nvidia's journey is marked by relentless innovation and strategic foresight. In its early years, the company focused on developing GPUs that significantly enhanced the visual experience for gamers and professionals. The release of the GeForce 256 in 1999, dubbed the world's first GPU, was a pivotal moment. This groundbreaking product introduced hardware transform and lighting to the consumer market, setting Nvidia apart from its competitors and establishing its reputation for cutting-edge technology.

As the gaming industry exploded in the early 2000s, Nvidia's GPUs became the gold standard, powering the most advanced games and driving the company's growth. However, Nvidia's leadership recognized the potential of their GPU technology beyond gaming. They saw an opportunity in the nascent field of parallel computing, where GPUs could be used to handle complex computational tasks that CPUs struggled with. This led to the development of the CUDA platform in 2006, allowing developers to leverage the parallel processing power of GPUs for a wide range of applications, from scientific research to financial modeling.

The true turning point for Nvidia came with the rise of artificial intelligence. The company's GPUs proved to be exceptionally well-suited for training deep neural networks, the foundation of modern AI. This capability positioned Nvidia as a critical player in the AI revolution. Companies across various sectors—from automotive to healthcare—began adopting Nvidia's technology to develop AI-driven solutions. The introduction of the Volta and later the Ampere architectures cemented Nvidia's dominance in the AI hardware market, providing unmatched performance and efficiency.

Nvidia's strategic pivot to AI and data centers paid off handsomely. By 2023, Nvidia's stock had soared 239%, and in 2024, it achieved a market capitalization of $3.019

trillion, surpassing Apple to become the second-largest publicly traded company in the US. This milestone was not just a testament to Nvidia's financial success but also an acknowledgment of its central role in shaping the future of technology.

The significance of Nvidia's rise extends far beyond its market valuation. Nvidia has become synonymous with AI innovation, driving advancements that impact every corner of society. In healthcare, Nvidia's AI technology is used for drug discovery and diagnostic imaging. In automotive, Nvidia's platforms power the development of autonomous vehicles. The company's influence is evident in scientific research, where its GPUs enable complex simulations and data analysis, accelerating discoveries in fields ranging from astrophysics to climate science.

Moreover, Nvidia's success has broader implications for the tech industry. It underscores the importance of adaptability and foresight in a rapidly evolving technological landscape. Nvidia's ability to identify and capitalize on emerging trends, such as the shift from traditional computing to AI, has been a key factor in its ascent. This adaptability, combined with a culture of innovation, has positioned Nvidia as a leader not only in hardware but also in the broader tech ecosystem.

Nvidia's journey from a GPU manufacturer to a leader in AI and deep learning is a story of vision, innovation, and strategic execution. Its rise signifies a transformative shift in the tech industry, heralding an era where AI plays a central role in shaping the future. As Nvidia continues to push the boundaries of what is possible, its impact on technology and society will undoubtedly grow, making it a pivotal force in the digital age.

Chapter 1

The Early Days

Founding of Nvidia

The story of Nvidia's inception is rooted in the rapidly evolving tech landscape of the early 1990s, a time marked by explosive growth in the personal computer market and an increasing demand for advanced graphics capabilities. Nvidia was founded in April 1993 by Jensen Huang, Chris Malachowsky, and Curtis Priem, three engineers with a shared vision of transforming the way graphics were handled on personal computers.

Jensen Huang, the charismatic and visionary leader who would go on to become the face of Nvidia, brought with him a wealth of experience from his tenure at LSI Logic and Advanced Micro Devices (AMD). His passion for graphics technology and his relentless drive were crucial in steering Nvidia through its formative years. Chris Malachowsky and Curtis Priem, both accomplished engineers, shared Huang's enthusiasm for pushing the boundaries of what was technically possible. Together, they formed a formidable team, each bringing unique skills and perspectives to the fledgling company.

The founders were united by a bold idea: to create a single-chip graphical accelerator that could handle real-time rendering of complex graphics. This was an ambitious goal, given the limitations of the existing technology and the competitive landscape dominated by established companies like Intel and ATI Technologies. However, Huang, Malachowsky, and Priem were undeterred. They believed that the increasing complexity of computer graphics, driven by the burgeoning video game industry and the growing demand for graphical user interfaces, presented a significant opportunity.

Initial Challenges and Breakthroughs

The early days of Nvidia were fraught with challenges. The trio faced the daunting task of securing funding, a critical component for any startup aiming to develop cutting-edge technology. They pitched their vision to various venture capitalists, emphasizing the potential of their graphics chip to revolutionize the industry. Their perseverance paid off when they secured initial funding from Sequoia Capital, a renowned venture capital firm known for its investments in successful tech companies.

With funding in place, Nvidia set up its first office in Sunnyvale, California. The team worked tirelessly, driven by a shared belief in their mission. However, the path to success was not smooth. Nvidia's first product, the NV1, was released in 1995. The NV1 was a multimedia accelerator that combined 2D and 3D graphics, audio, and I/O functionality on a single chip. While innovative, the NV1 faced several issues, including compatibility problems with industry-standard APIs and limited software support. As a result, it did not achieve commercial success.

Despite this setback, the NV1 laid the groundwork for future innovations. Nvidia learned valuable lessons from the NV1's shortcomings and used this knowledge to refine their approach. The company adopted a more focused strategy, dedicating its resources to developing a high-performance 3D graphics chip. This pivot was crucial and led to the development of the RIVA 128, released in 1997.

The RIVA 128 marked a significant breakthrough for Nvidia. Unlike its predecessor, the RIVA 128 was designed to be fully compatible with Microsoft's Direct3D API, which was becoming the industry standard for 3D graphics. This strategic alignment with industry standards, coupled with the RIVA 128's impressive performance, made it a commercial success. The RIVA 128 helped establish Nvidia as a serious contender in the graphics market, setting the stage for the company's future growth.

Key Players and Visionaries

Jensen Huang's leadership was instrumental in navigating Nvidia through its early challenges. Known for his technical expertise and business acumen, Huang's vision extended beyond the immediate goal of developing a successful graphics chip. He foresaw the broader applications of graphics processing units (GPUs) and their potential impact on various industries. Huang's ability to articulate this vision and inspire his team was a key factor in Nvidia's eventual success.

Chris Malachowsky, co-founder and senior vice president of engineering and operations, played a crucial role in the technical development of Nvidia's products. His background in electrical engineering and his experience at Hewlett-Packard provided him with the expertise needed to drive Nvidia's innovation. Malachowsky's contributions were instrumental in overcoming the technical challenges that Nvidia faced in its early years.

Curtis Priem, the third co-founder, brought with him extensive experience in chip design from his work at Sun Microsystems and IBM. Priem's expertise was vital in the development of Nvidia's early products. His knowledge of microprocessor design and architecture helped Nvidia create chips that were not only powerful but also efficient and cost-effective.

Beyond the founding trio, several other key figures contributed to Nvidia's early success. Among them was David Kirk, who joined Nvidia in 1997 and served as the company's chief scientist for many years. Kirk's contributions to GPU architecture and his work on the development of Nvidia's hardware were critical in establishing the company's technological leadership.

Another notable figure was Jen-Hsun "Jensen" Hsu, a key engineer who worked on the development of the GeForce 256, the world's first GPU. Released in 1999, the GeForce 256 represented a significant leap forward in graphics technology. It introduced hardware transform and lighting, features that dramatically improved the quality and performance of 3D graphics. The GeForce 256's success cemented Nvidia's reputation as an industry leader and laid the foundation for the company's future dominance.

Building a Culture of Innovation

From its inception, Nvidia cultivated a culture of innovation and risk-taking. The company's founders understood that staying ahead in the rapidly evolving tech industry required not only technical excellence but also a willingness to take bold risks. This culture was reflected in Nvidia's approach to product development, which emphasized rapid iteration and a willingness to learn from failures.

Nvidia's commitment to innovation was also evident in its approach to research and development. The company invested heavily in R&D, recognizing that continuous innovation was essential to maintaining its competitive edge. This investment paid off, leading to a steady stream of groundbreaking products and technologies that kept Nvidia at the forefront of the industry.

Early Partnerships and Collaborations

In addition to internal innovation, Nvidia's early success was bolstered by strategic partnerships and collaborations. The company forged alliances with key players in the tech industry, including Microsoft and Intel. These partnerships helped Nvidia gain access to new markets and technologies, accelerating its growth.

One of the most significant collaborations was with Microsoft, which played a crucial role in the development of Direct3D. Nvidia's alignment with Direct3D standards ensured that its products were compatible with a wide range of software applications, making them more attractive to developers and consumers alike. This strategic move helped Nvidia establish a strong foothold in the gaming market, which was rapidly expanding during the late 1990s and early 2000s.

The Road Ahead

The early days of Nvidia were characterized by a relentless pursuit of excellence and a clear vision for the future. The company's ability to navigate challenges, learn from failures, and capitalize on emerging opportunities set the stage for its remarkable ascent. With a strong foundation built on innovation, strategic partnerships, and visionary leadership, Nvidia was well-positioned to become a dominant force in the tech industry.

As the company moved into the new millennium, it continued to push the boundaries of what was possible with GPU technology. The lessons learned from its early experiences, combined with a steadfast commitment to innovation, would guide Nvidia through the next phases of its journey, leading to the groundbreaking achievements that would define its legacy.

Nvidia's early days were marked by a combination of visionary leadership, technical innovation, and strategic foresight. The company's founders and key players laid a strong foundation that enabled Nvidia to overcome initial challenges and achieve significant breakthroughs. This foundation would prove critical as Nvidia continued to evolve and expand, ultimately transforming the tech industry and redefining the future of computing.

Chapter 2

The Evolution of Chip Technology

Development of GPU Technology

The development of Graphics Processing Unit (GPU) technology has been a cornerstone of Nvidia's success. From its inception, Nvidia recognized the potential of GPUs to transform computing, moving beyond traditional Central Processing Units (CPUs) to handle complex graphical tasks with higher efficiency and performance. This realization drove the company's innovation and strategic direction, leading to breakthroughs that would revolutionize various industries.

In the mid-1990s, the personal computer market was burgeoning, and the demand for enhanced graphics capabilities was rising sharply. Graphics-intensive applications, particularly in gaming and professional visualization, required more processing power than what CPUs could provide. Nvidia's early focus on developing dedicated graphics accelerators laid the groundwork for the modern GPU.

The release of the GeForce 256 in 1999 marked a significant milestone in the evolution of GPU technology. Touted as the world's first GPU, the GeForce 256 introduced the concept of hardware transform and lighting (T&L). This innovation allowed for real-time rendering of complex 3D scenes, dramatically improving the visual quality and performance of graphics. The GeForce 256's ability to offload these tasks from the CPU to the GPU marked a paradigm shift in computing, enabling more immersive and realistic graphics.

Nvidia's commitment to advancing GPU technology did not stop there. The company continued to innovate with each subsequent generation of GPUs, introducing features such as programmable shading, improved texture handling, and increased memory bandwidth. These advancements were driven by a combination of cutting-edge hardware design and sophisticated software algorithms, ensuring that Nvidia's GPUs remained at the forefront of performance and capability.

How Nvidia's Chips Revolutionized Gaming

One of the most profound impacts of Nvidia's GPU technology has been in the gaming industry. From the early days of rudimentary graphics to the stunningly realistic visuals of modern games, Nvidia's chips have played a crucial role in pushing the boundaries of what is possible in gaming.

The GeForce 256, with its hardware T&L, set a new standard for gaming graphics. Games that took advantage of this technology could render detailed 3D environments with dynamic lighting and shadows, creating a more immersive experience for players. This leap in graphical fidelity not only enhanced the visual appeal of games but also opened up new possibilities for game design, allowing developers to create more complex and engaging worlds.

Following the success of the GeForce 256, Nvidia continued to innovate with the release of the GeForce 2 series in 2000. The GeForce 2 GPUs featured advanced pixel and vertex shaders, which allowed for more realistic textures and lighting effects. These enhancements enabled developers to create games with richer visuals and more intricate details, further raising the bar for gaming graphics.

The introduction of the GeForce 3 series in 2001 brought programmable shaders to the mainstream, revolutionizing game development. Programmable shaders allowed developers to write custom programs for the GPU, enabling more sophisticated effects such as bump mapping, reflections, and complex lighting. This flexibility empowered game developers to unleash their creativity, resulting in games with unprecedented levels of realism and artistic expression.

Nvidia's SLI (Scalable Link Interface) technology, introduced in 2004, further revolutionized gaming by allowing multiple GPUs to work together in a single system. SLI enabled gamers to achieve higher performance and better graphics quality by harnessing the power of two or more GPUs. This innovation catered to the growing demand for high-performance gaming rigs and reinforced Nvidia's position as a leader in the gaming market.

The launch of the GeForce 8 series in 2006 marked another significant advancement with the introduction of the unified shader architecture. Unlike previous GPUs, which had separate shader units for vertex and pixel processing, the unified architecture allowed all shader units to handle any type of shading task. This flexibility resulted in more efficient use of the GPU's resources, leading to better performance and more realistic graphics.

Nvidia's GPUs have also been at the forefront of supporting new gaming technologies, such as high dynamic range (HDR) lighting, real-time ray tracing, and virtual reality (VR). The introduction of real-time ray tracing with the GeForce RTX series in 2018 was a game-changer, enabling incredibly realistic lighting, shadows, and reflections. This technology, previously used only in high-end rendering for movies, brought cinematic quality visuals to real-time gaming.

Early Innovations and Market Positioning

Nvidia's early innovations were not limited to hardware advancements; the company also focused on developing software solutions that complemented its GPUs. The release of the CUDA (Compute Unified Device Architecture) platform in 2006 was a pivotal moment. CUDA allowed developers to leverage the parallel processing power of Nvidia's GPUs for a wide range of applications beyond graphics, such as scientific computing, data analysis, and machine learning.

CUDA transformed Nvidia's market positioning by opening up new markets and applications for its GPUs. Researchers and scientists across various fields adopted CUDA to accelerate their computations, leading to breakthroughs in areas such as climate modeling, molecular dynamics, and financial simulations. This diversification not only expanded Nvidia's customer base but also demonstrated the versatility and power of its GPU technology.

Nvidia's strategic partnerships and collaborations also played a crucial role in its market positioning. The company's close relationship with Microsoft, particularly its alignment with the Direct3D API, ensured that Nvidia's

GPUs were optimized for a wide range of applications and games. This compatibility made Nvidia's products the preferred choice for developers and gamers alike, further solidifying its market position.

In addition to its technical innovations, Nvidia's marketing and branding efforts contributed to its success. The company's "The Way It's Meant to Be Played" campaign, launched in the early 2000s, highlighted the superior gaming experience offered by Nvidia's GPUs. This campaign, along with strategic partnerships with game developers and publishers, helped establish Nvidia as the go-to brand for gaming enthusiasts.

Nvidia's ability to anticipate and respond to market trends was another key factor in its success. As the demand for high-definition video and 3D graphics grew, Nvidia was quick to develop solutions that met these needs. The company's early entry into the mobile GPU market with its Tegra series demonstrated its foresight in recognizing the potential of mobile computing and gaming.

The introduction of Nvidia's GeForce Experience software in 2013 further enhanced its market positioning. GeForce Experience provided gamers with tools to optimize their game settings, record gameplay, and update drivers seamlessly. This focus on improving the user experience helped Nvidia build a loyal customer base and differentiate itself from competitors.

By the mid-2010s, Nvidia had firmly established itself as a leader in the GPU market, with a reputation for delivering high-performance, innovative products. The company's strategic focus on research and development, coupled with its ability to adapt to changing market dynamics, positioned it for continued success.

The Road Ahead

As Nvidia moved into the latter half of the 2010s, its focus on innovation and market expansion continued to drive its growth. The company's entry into the data center and artificial intelligence (AI) markets opened up new opportunities and further diversified its revenue streams. Nvidia's GPUs, already known for their prowess in gaming, proved to be exceptionally well-suited for AI and machine learning tasks, solidifying the company's position as a leader in the tech industry.

Nvidia's evolution from a graphics card manufacturer to a dominant player in AI, gaming, and data centers is a testament to its ability to innovate and adapt. The company's commitment to pushing the boundaries of what is possible with GPU technology has had a profound impact on multiple industries, setting the stage for continued growth and success.

Nvidia's journey through the evolution of chip technology has been marked by relentless innovation, strategic foresight, and a deep understanding of market needs. From revolutionizing gaming graphics to pioneering advancements in AI and parallel computing, Nvidia's GPUs have consistently set new standards for performance and capability. As the company continues to explore new frontiers, its legacy of innovation and market leadership will undoubtedly endure, shaping the future of technology for years to come.

Chapter 3

Entering the AI Revolution

Transition from Gaming to AI

Nvidia's initial success was built on its pioneering work in the gaming industry, where its GPUs revolutionized the visual experience for gamers worldwide. However, the true transformative journey began when Nvidia recognized the broader potential of its GPU technology in fields beyond gaming, most notably in artificial intelligence (AI). This strategic pivot towards AI marked a significant evolution in the company's trajectory and reshaped its future.

The transition from gaming to AI was not an abrupt shift but a gradual and calculated move. Nvidia's foray into AI began with its understanding that the parallel processing capabilities of GPUs could be harnessed for more than just rendering graphics. GPUs excel at performing many calculations simultaneously, a feature that makes them highly suitable for training deep neural networks, the backbone of modern AI.

The introduction of CUDA (Compute Unified Device Architecture) in 2006 was a pivotal moment. CUDA allowed developers to program Nvidia GPUs for general-purpose computing, opening up new possibilities for scientific research, data analysis, and eventually, AI. Researchers and scientists quickly adopted CUDA for its ability to accelerate computationally intensive tasks, leading to significant breakthroughs in various fields.

Nvidia's GPUs became increasingly popular in AI research due to their unmatched performance in handling the massive computational demands of training deep learning models. Unlike traditional CPUs, which are designed for sequential processing, GPUs can process thousands of tasks concurrently. This capability is crucial for deep learning, where training models involves processing vast amounts of data and performing numerous complex calculations.

The Significance of AI in Modern Technology

AI has become a cornerstone of modern technology, influencing nearly every aspect of our lives. From powering voice assistants and recommendation systems to enabling autonomous vehicles and advancing medical diagnostics, AI's impact is profound and far-reaching. The rise of AI has been driven by the availability of vast datasets, advances in algorithms, and crucially, the computational power provided by GPUs.

Deep learning, a subset of AI, has particularly benefited from GPU technology. Deep learning models, inspired by the human brain's neural networks, require immense computational resources to process and learn from large datasets. GPUs, with their parallel processing capabilities, significantly accelerate this process, making it feasible to train complex models within reasonable timeframes.

The significance of AI in modern technology cannot be overstated. In healthcare, AI-powered diagnostic tools analyze medical images with remarkable accuracy, aiding in early disease detection and improving patient outcomes. In finance, AI algorithms detect fraudulent transactions and predict market trends. In manufacturing, AI optimizes production processes and enhances quality control. These applications, and many more, demonstrate how AI is transforming industries and driving innovation.

As AI continues to evolve, the demand for more powerful and efficient computing solutions grows. This demand has positioned Nvidia at the forefront of the AI revolution, as its GPUs provide the necessary computational horsepower to drive AI advancements. Nvidia's strategic shift towards AI was not just a response to market opportunities but also a recognition of the fundamental role that GPUs play in the AI ecosystem.

Nvidia's Strategic Shift Towards AI

Nvidia's strategic shift towards AI was guided by the visionary leadership of its CEO, Jensen Huang. Huang foresaw the transformative potential of AI and the critical role that Nvidia's technology could play in this new era. Under his guidance, Nvidia made significant investments in AI research and development, laying the foundation for its leadership in the AI market.

One of the earliest and most impactful steps in this direction was the launch of the Nvidia Tesla GPU in 2007. Designed specifically for high-performance computing (HPC) and scientific applications, the Tesla GPU provided unparalleled performance for AI and deep learning tasks. This product marked Nvidia's entry into the data center market, where AI workloads demanded exceptional computational power.

The acquisition of Mellanox Technologies in 2019 was another strategic move that bolstered Nvidia's position in AI. Mellanox, a leader in high-performance networking technology, complemented Nvidia's strengths in GPU computing. This acquisition enhanced Nvidia's ability to offer comprehensive AI solutions that integrated cutting-edge computing and networking capabilities, further solidifying its leadership in the data center market.

Nvidia's introduction of the Volta architecture in 2017 represented a significant leap forward in AI computing. The Volta GPUs featured Tensor Cores, specialized units designed to accelerate deep learning tasks. This innovation dramatically improved the performance and efficiency of AI training and inference, making Nvidia's GPUs even more attractive to researchers and enterprises developing AI applications.

The Ampere architecture, introduced in 2020, continued this trend with further enhancements in AI performance. Ampere GPUs delivered unprecedented levels of computational power, making them the preferred choice for AI workloads. The integration of AI-specific features, such as mixed-precision training and real-time ray tracing, underscored Nvidia's commitment to pushing the boundaries of what is possible in AI.

Nvidia's software ecosystem has also been a critical component of its AI strategy. The Nvidia Deep Learning Institute (DLI) offers training and resources to help developers harness the power of GPUs for AI. Nvidia's software libraries, such as cuDNN (CUDA Deep Neural Network library), provide optimized routines for AI and deep learning, making it easier for developers to build and deploy AI applications.

Furthermore, Nvidia's collaboration with industry leaders and research institutions has been instrumental in advancing AI technology. Partnerships with companies like Google, Microsoft, and Amazon have integrated Nvidia's GPUs into their AI cloud services, making powerful AI capabilities accessible to a broader audience. Collaborative research initiatives with top universities and research labs have driven innovation and expanded the boundaries of AI.

Nvidia's strategic shift towards AI has not only positioned the company as a leader in the AI market but has also had a profound impact on the broader tech industry. By providing the computational power necessary for AI advancements, Nvidia has enabled countless innovations that have transformed industries and improved lives.

The Broader Impact and Future Prospects

Nvidia's transition from gaming to AI is a testament to its ability to adapt and innovate in response to emerging opportunities. This strategic pivot has propelled Nvidia to new heights, with its GPUs becoming indispensable tools for AI researchers, developers, and enterprises worldwide.

The impact of Nvidia's technology extends beyond AI research to practical applications that are shaping the future. In autonomous driving, Nvidia's DRIVE platform provides the computational power and software needed to develop and deploy self-driving cars. In healthcare, Nvidia's Clara platform leverages AI to improve medical imaging, genomics, and drug discovery. These applications demonstrate how Nvidia's GPUs are driving advancements in critical areas that have a direct impact on society.

As AI continues to evolve, the demand for more powerful and efficient computing solutions will only grow. Nvidia's ongoing commitment to innovation positions it well to meet this demand and to continue leading the AI revolution. The company's focus on developing next-generation architectures, such as the upcoming Rubin platform, ensures that it remains at the cutting edge of AI technology.

Looking ahead, Nvidia's role in the AI ecosystem is likely to expand further. The convergence of AI with other emerging technologies, such as 5G, edge computing, and the Internet of Things (IoT), presents new opportunities for Nvidia to drive innovation. By integrating AI capabilities into these technologies, Nvidia can help unlock new possibilities and create value across diverse industries.

Nvidia's strategic shift towards AI has been a defining moment in the company's history. From its early days as a gaming graphics card manufacturer to its current position as a leader in AI computing, Nvidia's journey reflects its ability to anticipate and capitalize on technological trends.

As AI continues to reshape the world, Nvidia's contributions will remain pivotal, driving progress and enabling the next generation of technological breakthroughs.

Chapter 4

Breaking New Grounds: Key Milestones

Major Product Launches

Nvidia's journey to becoming a tech giant has been marked by numerous groundbreaking product launches that have reshaped industries and pushed the boundaries of what is possible with computing technology. These products, driven by relentless innovation and a commitment to excellence, have solidified Nvidia's reputation as a leader in the tech industry.

One of the most iconic product launches in Nvidia's history was the introduction of the GeForce 256 in 1999. Dubbed the world's first Graphics Processing Unit (GPU), the GeForce 256 revolutionized gaming graphics by introducing hardware transform and lighting (T&L) capabilities. This innovation laid the foundation for modern 3D gaming, setting a new standard for visual fidelity and performance.

Building on the success of the GeForce 256, Nvidia continued to push the envelope with subsequent generations of GPUs. The GeForce 2 series, released in

2000, introduced advanced pixel and vertex shaders, enabling more realistic lighting and texture effects. The GeForce 3 series, launched in 2001, brought programmable shaders to the mainstream, empowering game developers to create more immersive and visually stunning games.

Nvidia has also made significant strides in the data center and artificial intelligence (AI) markets. The introduction of the Nvidia Tesla GPU in 2007 marked the company's entry into the data center market, providing unparalleled performance for high-performance computing (HPC) and scientific applications. Subsequent generations of Tesla GPUs, such as the Volta and Ampere architectures, have further solidified Nvidia's position as a leader in AI computing.

Nvidia's product portfolio has also expanded to include solutions for autonomous driving, healthcare, and edge computing. The Nvidia DRIVE platform, introduced in 2015, provides the computational power and software needed to develop and deploy self-driving cars. The Nvidia Clara platform, launched in 2018, leverages AI to improve medical imaging, genomics, and drug discovery. These products demonstrate Nvidia's commitment to driving innovation across diverse industries.

Significant Partnerships and Collaborations

Nvidia's success is not just the result of its own innovations but also of strategic partnerships and collaborations with industry leaders and research institutions. These partnerships have enabled Nvidia to leverage complementary technologies and expertise, accelerating the development and adoption of its products.

One of Nvidia's most significant partnerships is with Microsoft, particularly in the gaming space. Nvidia's alignment with Microsoft's Direct3D API ensured that its GPUs were optimized for a wide range of gaming applications, making them the preferred choice for developers and gamers alike. Collaborations with game developers and publishers further strengthened Nvidia's position in the gaming market, establishing its GPUs as the gold standard for gaming graphics.

Nvidia has also forged partnerships with leading cloud providers, such as Amazon Web Services (AWS) and Google Cloud Platform (GCP), to offer GPU-accelerated computing services. These partnerships make Nvidia's GPUs accessible to a broader audience of developers and enterprises, enabling them to leverage the power of GPU computing for AI, scientific research, and other compute-intensive workloads.

In the automotive industry, Nvidia has partnered with automakers and Tier 1 suppliers to integrate its technology into autonomous vehicles. Collaborations with companies like Audi, Mercedes-Benz, and Volvo have led to the development of advanced driver assistance systems (ADAS) and autonomous driving solutions that rely on Nvidia's DRIVE platform.

Nvidia's collaborations extend beyond industry partnerships to include academic and research institutions. The company works closely with top universities and research labs to advance AI and GPU computing. These collaborations drive innovation and foster the development of cutting-edge technologies that benefit society as a whole.

Industry Recognition and Awards

Nvidia's groundbreaking products and strategic partnerships have been widely recognized by industry experts and organizations, earning the company numerous awards and accolades over the years. These accolades reflect Nvidia's commitment to excellence and innovation, as well as its significant contributions to the tech industry.

One of Nvidia's most prestigious awards is the IEEE Corporate Innovation Award, which the company received in 2017 for its contributions to the advancement of GPU computing and AI. This award recognizes Nvidia's pioneering work in developing GPU technology and its transformative impact on various industries.

Nvidia's GPUs have also been recognized for their exceptional performance and capabilities in gaming. The company has received multiple awards from leading gaming publications and organizations, including IGN, PC Gamer, and The Game Awards. These awards highlight Nvidia's commitment to delivering the best possible gaming experience for players worldwide.

In the AI and data center markets, Nvidia's products have received widespread acclaim for their unmatched performance and efficiency. The company's Tesla GPUs have been recognized by organizations such as Gartner and IDC for their leadership in HPC and AI computing. Nvidia's DGX systems, which integrate its GPUs with high-speed networking and software, have also received awards for their innovative design and performance.

Furthermore, Nvidia's efforts in the automotive industry have been recognized with awards for its DRIVE platform and autonomous driving solutions. The company has received accolades from industry organizations and publications for its contributions to the development of ADAS and self-driving technology.

, Nvidia's key milestones, including major product launches, strategic partnerships, and industry recognition, underscore the company's leadership and innovation in the tech industry. These achievements reflect Nvidia's unwavering commitment to pushing the boundaries of what is possible with computing technology and its dedication to driving progress and innovation across diverse industries.

Chapter 5

Financial Growth and Market Strategy

Analysis of Nvidia's Financial Performance

Nvidia's financial performance has been nothing short of remarkable, reflecting its status as a leader in the tech industry and its ability to capitalize on emerging opportunities. Over the years, Nvidia has consistently delivered strong revenue growth and profitability, driven by its innovative products and strategic market positioning.

One of the key indicators of Nvidia's financial success is its revenue growth. The company's revenue has experienced significant year-over-year growth, fueled by increasing demand for its GPUs across various industries. Nvidia's revenue growth can be attributed to several factors, including the growing popularity of gaming, the rise of AI and data center computing, and the expansion of its automotive and professional visualization businesses.

In addition to revenue growth, Nvidia has also demonstrated strong profitability. The company's gross margin, a measure of profitability, has remained consistently high, reflecting the value of its products and its ability to command premium prices. Nvidia's focus on high-performance, high-margin products, such as its gaming GPUs and data center solutions, has contributed to its strong profitability.

Nvidia's financial performance has also been characterized by prudent financial management and a focus on shareholder value. The company has maintained a healthy balance sheet, with ample cash reserves and low debt levels. Nvidia's disciplined approach to capital allocation, including share buybacks and strategic investments, has enhanced shareholder returns and bolstered investor confidence.

Key Strategies that Fueled Growth

Nvidia's remarkable financial growth can be attributed to several key strategies that have fueled its success. One of the most important strategies is the company's relentless focus on innovation. Nvidia has a long history of pushing the boundaries of what is possible with computing technology, consistently delivering industry-leading products that set new standards for performance and capability. By investing heavily in research and development, Nvidia has been able to stay ahead of the competition and maintain its leadership position in key markets.

Another key strategy that has fueled Nvidia's growth is its strategic market positioning. The company has successfully identified and capitalized on emerging trends and market opportunities, such as gaming, AI, and data center computing. Nvidia's early investments in these areas have allowed it to establish a strong foothold and capture significant market share, positioning it for continued growth as these markets continue to expand.

Nvidia's ecosystem approach to product development and marketing has also been instrumental in driving growth. The company has cultivated a broad ecosystem of partners, developers, and customers, leveraging these relationships to drive adoption of its products and technologies. By collaborating closely with industry partners and fostering a vibrant developer community, Nvidia has been able to accelerate innovation and drive market expansion.

Additionally, Nvidia's focus on vertical integration and differentiation has been a key driver of its growth. The company designs and manufactures its own GPUs, giving it greater control over product development and quality. Nvidia's vertical integration also allows it to offer end-to-end solutions, such as its DGX systems for AI and data center computing, which provide customers with a seamless and integrated experience.

Investment and Market Expansion

Nvidia's growth has been fueled in part by strategic investments and market expansion initiatives. The company has made targeted acquisitions and investments to expand its product portfolio and enter new markets. For example, Nvidia's acquisition of Mellanox Technologies in 2019 bolstered its position in the data center market and provided opportunities for synergies and innovation.

Nvidia has pursued organic growth through market expansion and diversification. The company has invested in research and development to develop new products and technologies that address emerging market needs. For example, Nvidia's expansion into the automotive market with its DRIVE platform has opened up new opportunities for growth and differentiation.

Nvidia has also focused on expanding its geographic footprint to tap into new markets and customer segments. The company has established a strong presence in key regions such as North America, Europe, and Asia, leveraging its global reach to drive sales and market penetration. By investing in sales and marketing initiatives and building relationships with local partners, Nvidia has been able to successfully expand its reach and capture market share in diverse markets around the world.

Looking ahead, Nvidia's growth prospects remain bright, fueled by its continued focus on innovation, strategic market positioning, and investment in growth initiatives. As emerging technologies such as AI, autonomous driving, and edge computing continue to gain traction, Nvidia is well-positioned to capitalize on these trends and drive continued financial growth and market leadership

Chapter 6

Competition and Market Dynamics

Nvidia vs. Other Tech Giants

Nvidia operates in a highly competitive landscape, facing competition from other tech giants across various segments of its business. In the gaming industry, Nvidia competes with companies like AMD and Intel, which also manufacture graphics processing units (GPUs) for gaming PCs and consoles. While Nvidia has traditionally dominated the high-end gaming market with its GeForce GPUs, AMD and Intel have been making strides in recent years, introducing competitive products that offer similar performance at lower price points.

In the data center and artificial intelligence (AI) markets, Nvidia faces competition from companies like Intel, AMD, and specialized AI hardware startups. Intel, in particular, has been ramping up its efforts to capture market share in the data center space, leveraging its expertise in CPU manufacturing to develop accelerators for AI and HPC workloads. Similarly, AMD has been investing in its GPU and CPU technology to target the data center market, posing a growing threat to Nvidia's dominance.

In the automotive industry, Nvidia competes with companies like Intel's Mobileye, Qualcomm, and Tesla, which develop their own autonomous driving technologies. While Nvidia's DRIVE platform is widely regarded as a leader in autonomous vehicle technology, competition in this space is intensifying as more companies enter the market and invest in developing their own self-driving solutions.

Competitive Landscape and Market Challenges

The competitive landscape in which Nvidia operates is characterized by rapid technological innovation, shifting market dynamics, and evolving customer demands. One of the key challenges Nvidia faces is the commoditization of its products, particularly in the gaming market. As competition intensifies and technology advances, it becomes increasingly difficult for Nvidia to differentiate its products and maintain premium pricing.

Another challenge for Nvidia is the emergence of new technologies and market trends that could disrupt its business model. For example, the rise of cloud gaming services and streaming platforms threatens to reduce the demand for high-end gaming hardware, impacting Nvidia's gaming GPU sales. Similarly, the growing popularity of AI-powered edge computing could shift demand away from traditional data center solutions, affecting Nvidia's data center business.

Intel's entry into the discrete GPU market poses a significant threat to Nvidia's dominance, particularly in the gaming and data center segments. With its vast resources and manufacturing capabilities, Intel has the potential to disrupt the GPU market and capture market share from Nvidia. Additionally, AMD's resurgence in recent years has put pressure on Nvidia to innovate and deliver competitive products across its product lines.

Strategies to Stay Ahead

To stay ahead of the competition and navigate the challenges of the market, Nvidia has adopted several strategic initiatives aimed at maintaining its leadership position and driving growth.

One of Nvidia's key strategies is to continue investing in research and development to develop cutting-edge technologies and innovative products. By staying at the forefront of technological innovation, Nvidia can differentiate its products and maintain a competitive edge in the market. The company's focus on developing AI and GPU technologies for emerging markets such as autonomous driving, healthcare, and edge computing positions it well to capitalize on future growth opportunities.

Nvidia also focuses on building strategic partnerships and collaborations with industry leaders to expand its reach and drive market adoption of its products. By working closely with partners across various industries, Nvidia can leverage their expertise and resources to accelerate product development and market penetration. Collaborations with cloud providers, automakers, and research institutions enable Nvidia to access new markets and customer segments, driving revenue growth and diversification.

Furthermore, Nvidia's focus on vertical integration and differentiation helps it maintain its competitive position in the market. By designing and manufacturing its own GPUs and developing proprietary software solutions, Nvidia can offer end-to-end solutions that deliver superior performance and value to customers. The company's ecosystem approach to product development and marketing, which includes partnerships with game developers, software vendors, and system integrators, further strengthens its competitive advantage and enhances customer loyalty.

Nvidia operates in a competitive market characterized by rapid technological change and evolving customer demands. By investing in research and development, building strategic partnerships, and focusing on vertical integration and differentiation, Nvidia can stay ahead of the competition and drive continued growth and innovation in the tech industry.

Chapter 7

AI and Deep Learning: The Game Changers

Nvidia's Contributions to AI and Deep Learning

Nvidia has been at the forefront of advancing artificial intelligence (AI) and deep learning, driving innovation and reshaping industries with its groundbreaking technologies and platforms. The company's contributions to AI and deep learning have been instrumental in accelerating the development and adoption of AI-powered applications and solutions across diverse industries.

One of Nvidia's most significant contributions to AI and deep learning is its development of high-performance GPUs optimized for parallel processing. GPUs are well-suited for training and running deep neural networks, the foundation of modern AI, due to their ability to perform thousands of calculations simultaneously. Nvidia's GPUs provide the computational power needed to train complex AI models on large datasets quickly and efficiently, enabling researchers and developers to explore new frontiers in AI research and application.

In addition to hardware innovations, Nvidia has also developed software platforms and tools to support AI and deep learning workflows. The Nvidia CUDA parallel computing platform and cuDNN (CUDA Deep Neural Network library) provide developers with the tools and libraries needed to accelerate AI and deep learning tasks on Nvidia GPUs. These software solutions enable researchers and developers to optimize their algorithms and achieve maximum performance on Nvidia's hardware.

Key AI Products and Platforms

Nvidia offers a range of products and platforms designed to accelerate AI and deep learning workflows and drive innovation across industries. One of Nvidia's flagship AI platforms is the Nvidia DGX system, a fully integrated AI supercomputing platform that delivers unprecedented computational power for AI research and development. The DGX system combines Nvidia's high-performance GPUs with optimized software and networking solutions to provide a turnkey solution for AI workloads.

Another key AI product from Nvidia is the Nvidia Tesla GPU, a series of high-performance GPUs optimized for data center and HPC applications. The Tesla GPUs are used to power AI inference and training tasks in data centers, enabling enterprises to deploy AI-powered solutions at scale. Nvidia's Tesla GPUs are also widely used in industries such as healthcare, finance, and automotive for applications such as medical imaging, financial modeling, and autonomous driving.

Nvidia's AI platforms extend beyond hardware to include software solutions and libraries that enable developers to build and deploy AI-powered applications more effectively. The Nvidia CUDA parallel computing platform, cuDNN library, and TensorRT inference optimizer provide developers with the tools and frameworks needed to accelerate AI and deep learning tasks on Nvidia GPUs. These software solutions enable developers to optimize their algorithms and achieve maximum performance on Nvidia's hardware.

Impact on Industries Beyond Tech

Nvidia's contributions to AI and deep learning have had a profound impact on industries beyond the tech sector, driving innovation and transforming traditional business models across diverse industries.

In healthcare, Nvidia's AI technologies are being used to accelerate medical imaging, drug discovery, and genomics research, enabling faster and more accurate diagnosis and treatment of diseases. AI-powered medical imaging solutions, powered by Nvidia's GPUs, are helping healthcare providers detect and diagnose conditions such as cancer, heart disease, and neurological disorders with greater accuracy and efficiency.

In finance, Nvidia's AI technologies are being used to analyze vast amounts of financial data and identify patterns and trends that can inform investment decisions and risk management strategies. AI-powered algorithms, running on Nvidia's GPUs, are helping financial institutions optimize trading strategies, detect fraud and money laundering, and assess credit risk more effectively.

In manufacturing, Nvidia's AI technologies are being used to optimize production processes, improve quality control, and enhance supply chain management. AI-powered computer vision systems, powered by Nvidia's GPUs, are helping manufacturers identify defects, monitor production lines, and automate tasks such as inventory management and logistics planning.

In transportation, Nvidia's AI technologies are being used to develop autonomous vehicles, improve traffic management systems, and enhance driver safety. AI-powered perception and navigation systems, powered by Nvidia's GPUs, are helping autonomous vehicles navigate complex environments, detect and avoid obstacles, and make real-time decisions to ensure safe and efficient transportation.

Nvidia's contributions to AI and deep learning have had a transformative impact on industries beyond the tech sector, driving innovation and reshaping traditional business models. By providing high-performance hardware and software solutions optimized for AI and deep learning, Nvidia has empowered researchers, developers, and enterprises to harness the power of AI and unlock new opportunities for growth and innovation across diverse industries.

Chapter 8

Surpassing Apple: A Historic Milestone

Events Leading Up to Surpassing Apple

Nvidia's historic achievement of surpassing Apple to become the second-largest publicly traded company in the US by market capitalization marked a significant milestone in the company's journey and reflected its growing influence and prominence in the tech industry.

The events leading up to this milestone were characterized by Nvidia's exceptional performance and market dominance, driven largely by the growing demand for its AI and GPU technologies. As the global economy rebounded from the challenges of the COVID-19 pandemic, Nvidia's stock price surged, propelled by strong quarterly earnings reports and bullish investor sentiment.

Nvidia's continued success in the AI and data center markets, coupled with its strategic acquisitions and partnerships, contributed to its rapid growth and rising market capitalization. The company's announcement of its most advanced AI chip platform, the Rubin platform, slated for rollout in 2026, further fueled investor optimism and confidence in Nvidia's long-term prospects.

Market Reaction and Implications

Nvidia's surpassing of Apple in market capitalization was met with widespread market reaction and implications, both within the tech industry and the broader financial markets. The news sent shockwaves through Wall Street, signaling a shifting of the guard in the hierarchy of tech giants and highlighting Nvidia's emergence as a formidable player in the industry.

The market reaction to Nvidia's achievement was largely positive, with Nvidia's stock price rallying on the news and reaching new record highs. Investors and analysts alike hailed the milestone as a testament to Nvidia's leadership and innovation, as well as a reflection of the company's growing influence in shaping the future of technology.

The implications of Nvidia's market capitalization surpassing Apple were far-reaching, signaling a seismic shift in the balance of power within the tech industry. While Apple remained the largest publicly traded company in the US by market capitalization, Nvidia's ascent to the second position underscored the growing importance of AI and GPU technologies in driving value and growth in the digital economy.

Detailed Analysis of the Market Cap Achievement

Nvidia's achievement of surpassing Apple in market capitalization was the culmination of years of strategic planning, execution, and innovation. A detailed analysis of this milestone reveals several key factors that contributed to Nvidia's success and market dominance.

First and foremost, Nvidia's leadership in AI and GPU technologies played a pivotal role in driving its market capitalization growth. The company's GPUs are widely regarded as best-in-class for AI and deep learning applications, powering everything from data centers to autonomous vehicles. Nvidia's dominance in these high-growth markets positioned it as a frontrunner in the race to capitalize on the AI revolution.

Second, Nvidia's strategic acquisitions and partnerships bolstered its market position and fueled its growth trajectory. The acquisition of Mellanox Technologies in 2019 expanded Nvidia's footprint in the data center market, while partnerships with leading cloud providers and automakers further solidified its leadership in AI and autonomous driving.

Third, Nvidia's commitment to innovation and product development differentiated it from its competitors and attracted investors seeking exposure to high-growth tech stocks. The company's announcement of the Rubin platform, its most advanced AI chip platform yet, underscored Nvidia's forward-thinking approach and its ability to anticipate and capitalize on emerging trends in the tech industry.

Nvidia's achievement of surpassing Apple in market capitalization was a historic milestone that underscored the company's growing influence and prominence in the tech industry. Driven by its leadership in AI and GPU technologies, strategic acquisitions and partnerships, and commitment to innovation, Nvidia positioned itself as a frontrunner in shaping the future of technology and driving value for investors.

Chapter 9

Technological Innovations and Patents

Significant Technological Advancements

Nvidia has been at the forefront of technological innovation, driving advancements in graphics processing units (GPUs), artificial intelligence (AI), and deep learning. These technological advancements have not only reshaped industries but also propelled Nvidia to the forefront of the tech industry.

One of the most significant technological advancements by Nvidia is the development of the CUDA parallel computing platform. CUDA enables developers to harness the computational power of Nvidia GPUs for parallel processing tasks, such as scientific simulations, data analysis, and AI training. This breakthrough technology revolutionized GPU computing and paved the way for Nvidia's dominance in the AI and data center markets.

Another groundbreaking innovation by Nvidia is its deep learning and AI technologies, which have transformed industries ranging from healthcare to finance. Nvidia's GPUs are widely used for training deep neural networks, the backbone of modern AI, enabling researchers and developers to tackle complex problems with unprecedented speed and accuracy. These AI technologies have led to breakthroughs in medical imaging, drug discovery, autonomous driving, and more, revolutionizing the way we live and work.

Key Patents and Their Impact on the Industry

Nvidia holds a vast portfolio of patents covering a wide range of technologies, from GPU architectures to AI algorithms. These patents are instrumental in protecting Nvidia's intellectual property and ensuring its competitive advantage in the tech industry. Several key patents have had a significant impact on the industry and have paved the way for Nvidia's success.

One notable patent is Nvidia's invention of the unified shader architecture, which revolutionized the design of GPUs and enabled more flexible and efficient processing of graphics and compute workloads. This patented technology has been incorporated into Nvidia's GPU architectures, such as the GeForce, Quadro, and Tesla series, driving performance improvements and enabling new applications across diverse industries.

Another important patent is Nvidia's development of GPU-accelerated computing, which leverages the parallel processing capabilities of GPUs to accelerate a wide range of computational tasks. This patented technology has been widely adopted in industries such as finance, healthcare, and automotive, where the computational power of GPUs is used to accelerate AI, simulation, and data analysis workloads.

Innovations Driving Future Growth

Looking ahead, Nvidia continues to innovate and develop new technologies that will drive future growth and shape the future of computing. One area of focus is AI and deep learning, where Nvidia is investing heavily in developing next-generation AI chips and platforms. The company's upcoming Rubin platform, slated for rollout in 2026, promises to deliver unprecedented levels of performance and efficiency for AI workloads, further cementing Nvidia's leadership in the AI market.

Another area of innovation for Nvidia is autonomous driving, where the company's DRIVE platform is powering the development of self-driving cars and trucks. Nvidia's AI-powered perception and navigation systems, coupled with its high-performance GPUs, are enabling autonomous vehicles to navigate complex environments safely and efficiently. As the demand for autonomous driving technology continues to grow, Nvidia is poised to capitalize on this trend and drive future growth in the automotive market.

Additionally, Nvidia is exploring new frontiers in computing, such as edge computing and quantum computing, where the company's expertise in parallel processing and AI technologies can be leveraged to solve complex problems and drive innovation. By continuing to innovate and push the boundaries of what is possible with computing technology, Nvidia is well-positioned to drive future growth and shape the future of the tech industry.

In conclusion, Nvidia's technological innovations and patents have played a pivotal role in driving its success and shaping the future of computing. From GPU architectures to AI algorithms, Nvidia's innovations have revolutionized industries and propelled the company to the forefront of the tech industry. Looking ahead, Nvidia's continued focus on innovation and development will drive future growth and solidify its position as a leader in the digital economy.

Chapter 10

The Rubin Platform and Beyond

Introduction of the Rubin AI Chip Platform

Nvidia's announcement of the Rubin AI chip platform marked a significant milestone in the company's journey and underscored its commitment to pushing the boundaries of artificial intelligence (AI) and deep learning. The Rubin platform, slated for rollout in 2026, promises to deliver unprecedented levels of performance and efficiency, further solidifying Nvidia's leadership in the AI market.

The Rubin platform builds upon the success of previous AI chip platforms developed by Nvidia, such as the Blackwell platform. While the Blackwell platform was hailed as the "world's most powerful chip" upon its announcement in March, the Rubin platform aims to surpass it in terms of performance, efficiency, and versatility. By leveraging cutting-edge technologies and innovations, Nvidia aims to address the growing demand for AI computing solutions across diverse industries.

Comparison with Previous Platforms like Blackwell

The Rubin platform represents a significant advancement over previous platforms like Blackwell, offering enhanced performance, efficiency, and scalability. One of the key improvements of the Rubin platform is its increased computational power, enabling faster and more accurate AI training and inference tasks. The Rubin platform also boasts improved energy efficiency, allowing for more efficient use of resources and lower operating costs.

In addition to performance and efficiency improvements, the Rubin platform offers enhanced versatility and flexibility, making it suitable for a wide range of AI applications and workloads. Unlike previous platforms that were optimized for specific use cases, the Rubin platform is designed to be adaptable and customizable, allowing developers to tailor it to their specific needs and requirements.

Another key difference between the Rubin platform and previous platforms like Blackwell is its architecture and design. The Rubin platform leverages advanced semiconductor technologies and design methodologies to achieve higher levels of integration, performance, and reliability. By incorporating innovations such as advanced packaging techniques, novel materials, and optimized circuit designs, Nvidia has been able to push the boundaries of what is possible with AI chip platforms.

Future Prospects and Industry Expectations

The introduction of the Rubin platform has generated significant excitement and anticipation within the tech industry, with analysts and industry experts lauding its potential to drive innovation and reshape industries. Industry expectations for the Rubin platform are high, with many predicting that it will set new benchmarks for AI computing performance and efficiency.

One of the key areas of focus for the Rubin platform is autonomous driving, where the demand for AI computing solutions continues to grow. Nvidia's DRIVE platform, powered by the Rubin platform, promises to deliver breakthrough performance and capabilities for autonomous vehicles, enabling safer and more efficient transportation systems. Additionally, the Rubin platform is expected to find applications in healthcare, finance, manufacturing, and other industries where AI is increasingly being used to drive innovation and growth.

Looking ahead, the Rubin platform has the potential to redefine the future of computing and unlock new opportunities for growth and innovation. By providing developers and enterprises with access to cutting-edge AI computing technologies, Nvidia aims to accelerate the adoption of AI-powered solutions and drive value for its customers and partners.

The introduction of the Rubin platform represents a significant milestone in Nvidia's journey and underscores the company's commitment to advancing AI and deep learning. With its enhanced performance, efficiency, and versatility, the Rubin platform is poised to drive future growth and shape the future of the tech industry. As industry expectations continue to grow, Nvidia remains at the forefront of AI innovation, driving progress and reshaping industries with its groundbreaking technologies and platforms.

Chapter 11

Corporate Culture and Leadership

Role of Leadership in Nvidia's Success

Nvidia's success can be attributed in large part to the vision, leadership, and strategic guidance provided by its executive team. Under the leadership of CEO Jensen Huang, Nvidia has transformed from a niche graphics chip manufacturer to a global technology powerhouse, driving innovation and shaping the future of computing.

Jensen Huang's leadership style is characterized by his passion for technology, his relentless pursuit of excellence, and his commitment to fostering a culture of innovation and collaboration. As the co-founder and CEO of Nvidia, Huang has played a pivotal role in guiding the company through periods of rapid growth and transformation, steering it towards new opportunities and markets while staying true to its core values and principles.

In addition to Jensen Huang, Nvidia's executive team includes seasoned industry veterans and visionary leaders who have played instrumental roles in the company's success. Leaders such as Colette Kress, Nvidia's CFO, and

Jeff Fisher, head of Nvidia's gaming business, have helped shape Nvidia's strategic direction and drive growth in key markets.

Corporate Culture and Values

Nvidia's corporate culture is characterized by a strong sense of purpose, a commitment to excellence, and a passion for innovation. At the heart of Nvidia's culture are its core values, which include customer obsession, innovation, integrity, and teamwork. These values guide every aspect of the company's operations, from product development to customer service, and serve as a compass for decision-making and behavior.

Nvidia's culture of innovation is evident in its relentless pursuit of breakthrough technologies and solutions that push the boundaries of what is possible with computing. The company encourages employees to think creatively, take risks, and challenge the status quo, fostering an environment where new ideas are welcomed and nurtured.

Integrity is another key pillar of Nvidia's corporate culture, reflected in its commitment to ethical business practices, transparency, and accountability. Nvidia prioritizes honesty, fairness, and respect in all its dealings, building trust with customers, partners, and stakeholders.

Teamwork is also central to Nvidia's culture, with employees encouraged to collaborate across teams and disciplines to solve complex problems and drive innovation. Nvidia fosters a supportive and inclusive work environment where diversity is celebrated, and everyone has the opportunity to contribute and succeed.

Profiles of Key Leaders and Their Contributions

Jensen Huang, co-founder and CEO of Nvidia, is widely regarded as a visionary leader who has played a pivotal role in shaping the company's success. Huang's leadership has been characterized by his bold vision for the future of computing, his relentless focus on innovation, and his ability to inspire and motivate employees to achieve their full potential.

Colette Kress, Nvidia's CFO, is responsible for overseeing the company's financial strategy and operations. Kress has played a key role in driving Nvidia's growth and profitability, managing its finances and investments effectively, and providing strategic guidance to the executive team.

Jeff Fisher, head of Nvidia's gaming business, is responsible for overseeing the company's gaming products and services. Fisher's leadership has been instrumental in driving Nvidia's gaming business to new heights, expanding its reach and market share, and delivering innovative products and experiences to gamers around the world.

In addition to these key leaders, Nvidia's executive team includes a diverse group of talented individuals with expertise in areas such as engineering, marketing, and operations. Together, they form a cohesive and high-performing team that is committed to driving Nvidia's success and delivering value to its customers and shareholders.

Nvidia's success is the result of strong leadership, a vibrant corporate culture, and a relentless commitment to innovation and excellence. Under the guidance of visionary leaders like Jensen Huang, Nvidia has established itself as a global technology leader, driving progress and shaping the future of computing. As the company continues to grow and evolve, its leadership and corporate culture will remain key drivers of its success.

Chapter 12

Global Impact and Market Presence

Nvidia's Global Expansion

Nvidia's journey from a Silicon Valley startup to a global technology powerhouse is a testament to its relentless pursuit of innovation and strategic vision. Over the years, Nvidia has expanded its presence to become a key player in the global technology industry, with operations spanning across continents and serving customers in diverse markets.

Nvidia's global expansion strategy has been driven by its focus on key growth areas such as artificial intelligence (AI), data center computing, gaming, and autonomous driving. The company has established a strong presence in regions such as North America, Europe, Asia-Pacific, and Latin America, leveraging its expertise and technology leadership to address the unique needs and requirements of each market.

Market Presence in Various Regions

Nvidia's market presence in various regions reflects its commitment to serving customers and driving innovation on a global scale. In North America, Nvidia has a strong presence in Silicon Valley, where it is headquartered, as well as in major tech hubs such as Seattle, Austin, and Boston. The company's data center solutions are widely adopted by leading enterprises and cloud providers in the region, driving growth and innovation in areas such as AI, HPC, and cloud computing.

In Europe, Nvidia has established a significant presence in key markets such as the United Kingdom, Germany, France, and the Nordic countries. The company's AI and GPU technologies are powering a wide range of applications across industries such as automotive, healthcare, finance, and manufacturing, driving digital transformation and economic growth.

In the Asia-Pacific region, Nvidia has a strong presence in countries such as China, Japan, South Korea, and India. The company's gaming business is particularly popular in the region, with Nvidia GPUs powering gaming PCs and consoles in millions of households. Additionally, Nvidia's AI and data center solutions are driving innovation in industries such as e-commerce, fintech, and telecommunications, fueling growth and competitiveness in the region.

In Latin America, Nvidia's presence is growing rapidly, driven by increasing demand for AI and GPU technologies in emerging markets such as Brazil, Mexico, and Argentina. The company's investments in education, research, and development are helping to build local talent and expertise, driving innovation and economic development in the region.

Impact on Global Technology Standards

Nvidia's technology leadership and innovation have had a significant impact on global technology standards, shaping the way we live, work, and interact with technology. The company's GPUs have become the de facto standard for graphics processing and parallel computing, powering everything from high-end gaming PCs to supercomputers.

Nvidia's AI and deep learning technologies have also set new benchmarks for performance and efficiency, driving advancements in areas such as natural language processing, computer vision, and autonomous systems. The company's contributions to open-source software and hardware standards have further cemented its role as a leader in the global technology ecosystem, driving collaboration and innovation across industries.

In addition to setting new standards for performance and efficiency, Nvidia's technologies have also played a key role in enabling new applications and experiences that were previously unimaginable. From AI-powered medical imaging to real-time ray tracing in gaming, Nvidia's innovations have pushed the boundaries of what is possible with computing, inspiring new possibilities and driving progress in the digital age.

Nvidia's global impact and market presence reflect its leadership and innovation in the technology industry. Through strategic expansion, market presence in diverse regions, and contributions to global technology standards, Nvidia has established itself as a driving force in shaping the future of computing and driving progress on a global scale. As the company continues to grow and evolve, its global impact will continue to shape the way we live, work, and interact with technology in the years to come.

Chapter 13

The Future of Nvidia and AI

Predictions for Nvidia's Future Growth

Nvidia's future growth prospects look promising, fueled by continued advancements in artificial intelligence (AI), data center computing, gaming, and autonomous driving. As the demand for AI and GPU technologies continues to soar, Nvidia is well-positioned to capitalize on emerging opportunities and drive innovation across diverse industries.

One key area of growth for Nvidia is the data center market, where the company's AI and GPU technologies are powering a wide range of applications such as AI inference, HPC, and cloud computing. With the increasing adoption of AI and deep learning solutions in industries such as healthcare, finance, and manufacturing, Nvidia's data center business is poised for significant growth in the coming years.

Another area of growth for Nvidia is the gaming market, where the company's GPUs are widely regarded as best-in-class for high-performance gaming experiences. With the continued popularity of gaming and the rise of new gaming platforms such as cloud gaming and virtual reality, Nvidia's gaming business is expected to continue growing and driving revenue for the company.

Additionally, Nvidia's investments in autonomous driving technology are expected to drive future growth, as the demand for self-driving cars and trucks continues to rise. Nvidia's DRIVE platform, powered by its AI and GPU technologies, is leading the way in enabling autonomous vehicles to navigate complex environments safely and efficiently, paving the way for a future where transportation is safer, greener, and more efficient.

Emerging Trends in AI and Technology

Several emerging trends are shaping the future of AI and technology, presenting both challenges and opportunities for Nvidia and the industry as a whole. One key trend is the increasing convergence of AI and edge computing, where AI algorithms are being deployed directly on devices such as smartphones, IoT devices, and autonomous vehicles. This trend presents new opportunities for Nvidia to deliver AI solutions that are optimized for edge deployment, enabling real-time processing and decision-making in resource-constrained environments.

Another emerging trend is the growing demand for AI-powered healthcare solutions, driven by the need to improve patient outcomes, reduce costs, and enhance the efficiency of healthcare delivery. Nvidia's AI technologies are well-suited for applications such as medical imaging, drug discovery, and personalized medicine, where the company's GPUs are used to accelerate computational tasks and analyze large datasets.

Additionally, the rise of AI-powered virtual assistants and conversational AI is transforming the way we interact with technology, enabling more natural and intuitive user experiences. Nvidia's AI technologies are powering virtual assistants and chatbots that can understand and respond to human speech, enabling new possibilities for communication and interaction.

Potential Challenges and Opportunities

While Nvidia's future prospects are bright, the company also faces several challenges and opportunities as it continues to grow and evolve. One potential challenge is the increasing competition in the AI and GPU markets, with rivals such as Intel, AMD, and specialized AI hardware startups vying for market share. Nvidia will need to continue innovating and differentiating its products to stay ahead of the competition and maintain its leadership position.

Another potential challenge is the growing complexity and ethical considerations surrounding AI and deep learning technologies. As AI becomes more pervasive in our daily lives, concerns about privacy, bias, and accountability are becoming increasingly important. Nvidia will need to navigate these challenges carefully and ensure that its AI technologies are developed and deployed responsibly, with a focus on fairness, transparency, and accountability.

Despite these challenges, Nvidia also faces significant opportunities for growth and expansion in the years ahead. The continued adoption of AI and GPU technologies across industries presents new opportunities for Nvidia to drive innovation and deliver value to its customers and partners. By staying true to its core values of innovation, integrity, and teamwork, Nvidia can continue to shape the future of AI and technology and drive progress in the digital age.

In conclusion, the future of Nvidia and AI is bright, with opportunities for growth and innovation abound. By staying at the forefront of technological innovation, embracing emerging trends, and addressing potential challenges responsibly, Nvidia can continue to drive progress and shape the future of computing for years to come.

Conclusion

Nvidia's journey from a small graphics chip manufacturer to a global technology powerhouse is a testament to its relentless pursuit of innovation, commitment to excellence, and visionary leadership. Over the years, Nvidia has transformed industries, pushed the boundaries of what is possible with computing, and shaped the future of technology in profound ways.

At the heart of Nvidia's success is its unwavering dedication to advancing artificial intelligence (AI) and graphics processing unit (GPU) technologies. By pioneering breakthroughs in AI research, developing high-performance GPUs, and delivering innovative solutions to customers around the world, Nvidia has established itself as a leader in the AI revolution.

Nvidia's impact extends far beyond the tech industry, with its technologies powering applications and experiences that touch every aspect of our lives. From AI-powered medical imaging and autonomous driving to high-performance gaming and supercomputing, Nvidia's innovations have reshaped industries, transformed businesses, and improved the way we live, work, and interact with technology.

One of the key drivers of Nvidia's success is its corporate culture, which fosters a spirit of innovation, collaboration, and integrity. From CEO Jensen Huang to every employee, Nvidia is united by a shared vision of pushing the boundaries of what is possible with technology and delivering value to customers and partners.

Looking ahead, Nvidia's future is bright, with opportunities for growth and innovation abound. As the demand for AI and GPU technologies continues to soar, Nvidia is well-positioned to capitalize on emerging opportunities and drive progress in the digital age. By staying true to its core values of innovation, integrity, and teamwork, Nvidia can continue to shape the future of computing and drive progress on a global scale.

In conclusion, Nvidia's journey is a testament to the power of innovation, leadership, and perseverance. From its humble beginnings to its current position as a global technology leader, Nvidia has overcome challenges, seized opportunities, and reshaped industries with its groundbreaking technologies and solutions. As we look to the future, Nvidia's legacy will continue to inspire generations of innovators and shape the way we live, work, and interact with technology for years to come.

www.ingramcontent.com/pod-product-compliance
Lightning Source LLC
Chambersburg PA
CBHW070119230526
45472CB00004B/1338